THE ENGLISH SUMMER

Holly Hopkins grew up in Berkshire, grew up even more in London and now lives in Manchester. Her debut pamphlet, *Soon Every House Will Have One*, won the Poetry Business Pamphlet Competition and was the Poetry Book Society Pamphlet Choice. Holly has been an assistant editor of *The Rialto*. She has received an Eric Gregory Award and a Hawthornden Fellowship and was shortlisted for the inaugural Women Poets' Prize. Her poems featured in *Carcanet New Poetries VIII* and have been published in *The Guardian*, *The Telegraph* and *TLS*.

ALSO BY HOLLY HOPKINS

Soon Every House Will Have One (Smith|Doorstop, 2014)

The English Summer

HOLLY HOPKINS

Penned in the Margins
LONDON

PUBLISHED BY PENNED IN THE MARGINS
Toynbee Studios, 28 Commercial Street, London E1 6AB
www.pennedinthemargins.co.uk

First published 2022

Printed in the United Kingdom by TJ Books Ltd

ISBN
978-1-908058-94-2

CONTENTS

for Alex

The English Summer

Country Churches

They slip their moorings in the night
and glide down tarmac roads
to a city where evangelicals
are taking over bingo halls, old cinemas,
calling, singing, hot in electric light.

The English Summer

Dun-coloured endangered species of specialist interest;
best found on grungy paths, behind gabardines,
near shoes on school radiators, wet socks at work.
A furred creature, hood-hidden, brolly-blinded, shy.

The invasive species: a fearsome firestorm
of peeled blue sky. Allelopathic leaf-crisper,
river-fading grass-bleacher, ice-cream smiling
skin-killer, furze-burning forest-eater, agricide.

See the burn-blisters on the ridge of this ear.
See water rationing. See heat oedema. See dizziness.

Drought

In this version of St George
the horse is pissed off.

It's a horse with angry eyebrows.
It's a horse about to brain a dragon
with a hoof like a bag of nails.

George is pie-faced,
sword raised and forgotten;
he might as well be holding a balloon.

Hear the blade score
the lowest branches of the almond trees,
each bandaged white to the waist
with a plastic drip at the root.

The dragon's a Venus flytrap
with a snake body
that squeezes electric cars
until their sunrooves pop off.

This horse is livid.
This horse remembers the story:

a spring where water sobbed
from the earth,
fern-garnished and clear.

Enough to water
the golf courses of northern California.

The Death of a Fridge

Poured on skin, lighter fluid
burns shallow. My hand in flames
was no worse than a plaster ripped off;
we were more burnt by the sun.

I can't even remember his name.
He had a newspaper rolled in a torch
burning up too quick
and nowhere to drop it,
so we slammed it in the fridge.

The box sealed. The rubber trim
sucked tight. We couldn't force it
anymore than we could pull apart
a dinner plate. Not crack a dish
but hold the rims and pull it in two.
Everything has its own way to break.

The air was eaten: a dimple

in the cool enamel, a crease,
then, drawn from the inside,
the whole white weight crumpled
with thunks of deep struck metal,
as a girl, trapped by an earthquake,
might smash keys on a pipe
when she still thinks of rescue.

A Stone Wall Around The Duke of Northumberland's Park

You didn't think a private wall could be so long.
It cuts through rain-toughened sheep fields,
clay clubbed lulls, into cattle streams,
past thunderclouds of gorse.

After three uphill miles, you find a door
with a jagged hole the size of your hand.
You can't resist pressing your face to see:
more moor, more heather, a few black birch.

What you can't know is the wall from the other side.
What the Duke could've painted: those seaside boards
with a fat/thin couple and an oval for your face.

What do your hands look like from over there?
What speech balloon slips tail-first into your mouth?

Scuts

The rabbits' downy tails mark them
as one of nature's grass digesters,
the ones who hang sag-necked from foxes' jaws,
who lollop when attempting speed.
The ones whose side-face eyes
are trying to see both sides of the horizon,
who plug away inches from the earth
and never thought to lick warm blood.
Animals the colour of the underbrush
whose white butts flash in Morse distress,
strobe lights as they start to run,
saying, *I'm here! Dinner!* Seeming stupid,
until the patches of the hill you never saw
were breathing move as one, unraveling
the ground ahead in a white-capped rush.

Telephone Girls

Girls have always been joined to telephone systems.
Not just teenage gossips or 1940s' girls
in whale-fat lipstick, scalps smelling
of chemical burns for days after each perm,
girls plugged into circuit boards, primed for scandal,
heavy Bakelite ear cones and mouthpieces rising
like snakes' heads up from their breasts;
that's not what I mean.
I mean anchorites – telephones to God.

They chose to be built into church walls –
Dame Julian of Norwich;
Emma of All Saints, North Street, York –
the masonry rising like a slow upward guillotine.
The engineers would leave a slot
to admit a parcel of light and air,
food and requested prayers.

They believed that in this pure removal

they'd become a prayer machine.
That each day of silence would be another stitch
sewing their lips and ears into the robes of God
until their tears would fall directly in his lap.

The Flayings

A detergent cup of glue
waits in a flat-roofed primary school.
Your probing fingers dip,
find dry PVA peels off in strips,
membranes holding
a crazed pattern of skin.
Or it can be rubbed off,
dropping smuts like those left
when rubbing out mistakes. It escalates

to a childhood fascination with flame,
the slow seduction of wax,
tipping the candle to encourage long
lines to slip down, to puddle.
Your knuckle picks up a small white helmet
which can be removed when set.
This hurts. Now we're ready for skin.

A flash-roast summer, strappy tops

and our flesh scarlet by tea time.
When we wash off the day
our skin comes away in white webbing,
leaving nibbled coastlines, red islands.
We burn that night in our beds.

You'd think that would prepare us
for the day we stand in a lift
and see ourselves in the back-wall mirror,
the canned light bloating us like drowned things.
This soft pudge, our full inventory.
No more waiting to split out of a shell.

After the Workshops I'm Shown Round by a Member of Staff

'When Rapunzel became twelve, she turned into a very beautiful young girl so the fairy decided to lock her up in a tower… because that's apparently what you do with beautiful girls.'

JEN CAMPBELL, 'The History of Rapunzel', *Fairy Tales with Jen*

He wants to show me the five-a-side pitch,
he's been yearning to show me all day.
So, we walk around its crisp white edge
and I ask how often the kids get to play?
He does a double-take;
the children aren't allowed out here.

The Secure Children's Home has air-lock
breeze-block corridors
and uncrackable sheets of window.
The Secure Children's Home is more secure
than many official prisons
and I've seen a few.

He says, *Maybe the lads smashed up their rooms.*
Maybe they got into fights.
When other homes can't keep them on
they get sent here.

And the girls?
He says,
You've seen them.

He has to explain it to me.

They were slumped up in class,
playing with their long-groomed hair,
their impractical, childish hair.

He says,
Nobody wants another Rochdale.

Green Man in Spring

There's something in my teeth.
A thread of cress? A beansprout?
I have the urge to cough, little
chuffs, an engine failing to catch
growing to a dark wet hack

until I'm bent clutching my thighs,
choking up a swell in my throat.
I hook my finger in and pull
a damp wad of pondweed,
hair from a plughole,

when I feel a kind of worm,
probe up under my tongue
and I can see it just under my nose –
white, flailing. I try to rip it
but it's like thick plastic; it stretches

turning green, then pops up leaves

easy as umbrellas, heart-shaped bindweed
crawling on my face, up my ears,
over my forehead and as I reach
I feel the crown's white megaphone blooms.

Lady Godiva

It's lucky she has hair like frothy seaweed
that rolls around the sea like it is hair
but now she's standing naked in the courtyard
it sticks to skin like swathes of sweated chard
so her genitals are shielded by damp greens.

She dressed the horse with clanking brass and bells
and she's quietly stepping off the mounting block.
If all of Coventry will turn their backs
and focus on the whitewash down the wall,
or painted cloths if they are burghers' daughters,
or crusts of daub if they are bootless poor,
then she doesn't really need to ride the horse
and anyway the beast is flint and muscle
with a bag of broken knuckles in its mouth.

Later she will learn where Peeping Tom lives
and use a hatpin on him while he sleeps.

Zombies

We thought they'd be flesh-robots
with dowsing rod arms, relentless.
But when they rose they were so tired,
just wanted to rest up,
wet wood against a wall,
dummies from a damp museum.
They were excellent listeners.
There were plans to pair them
with the lonely and the elderly,
designated benches for them to chat,
but what little vim they had ran down.
We forgot about the cremated –
to be as light as dust.
A single fleck of soil nudged
and then another, miles away.
It took time, but sped up
around the iron filing stage.
Then the swarm:
each individual a brown cloud, no body, no brain,

no dead-weight-arms, no suitcase of meat.
Ever been in a sandstorm?
It feels like being bitten, at first,
then burned. They blew right through us.

Tidal Islands

Come tour this park with its two bright playgrounds,
a pets' corner, warm sourdough in the café,
the long rock garden shaded by jumbo conifers,
a scout hut in a former stable block,
a portly chestnut avenue, a lawn
where Queen Victoria once graced a garden fête,
a bowling green, a friends' scheme, a disc golf course,
a community orchard and a walled allotment club.
In the very centre is a row of well-proportioned red-brick villas
that just won't sell. The estate agents don't get it.

Rightmove shows the rooms are generous and immaculate:
cottagecore with mod-cons, good catchment areas,
professional part of the city, excellent transport links,
Farrow and Ball loft conversions, light wells, ensuites,
beaming bay windows, a greenhouse in the garden.
Daytime privacy is ensured by charming hedges.
At night, the park is a soft dark lake.
Midwinter, the sun sets at 3.48.

Remember keys warming in your fist
like the policeman showed you
in the special "only for girls" talk at school.

The City Cut from a Mountain

We waited for the windiest day to burn the forest,
flame handed from branch to waving branch.
High-pressure hoses cleared the soil,
the loose shale, until it was naked as an egg.

Then lasers, drills, giant crunching worms,
sand-blasters, down and in;
it made a ringed city, with a spiral road
that opened gently as a paper flower in water.

The houses were for us, winners of a lottery.
We left the broken glass of the old city,
that bowl of smog between chalk hills,
to live inside high granite walls.

In summer the rock was cool.
In winter, water from hot springs
was forced through drilled capillaries
until our houses shone with warmth.

That first New Year we built bonfires
on our rooves, cooked sausages on sticks,
wore our city uniforms of white wool.
Everything was fixed. Everyone fitted.

If you had two kids you had two bedrooms.
Later, if you had two bedrooms you had two kids.
In some studio flats, they found children
carved from the rock, polished red stone.

The Garden Cemetery Trust

Barbara cherishes the woods,
glossy hoardings, sprung bracken,
vegetable bric-a-brac.
In summer gloom the laurel leaves
are angels' military feathers.

Rachel knows that time is running out.
Industrious roots topple industrial monuments.
Lead lettering decays, iconoclastic climbers
slight essential columns.

Rachel gathers Saturday volunteers.
She hands out secateurs and folding saws.

Barbara writes to absent members
and steers elections to the board.

Rachel admires Tower Hamlets,
who mixed sand with topsoil,

beggaring the earth, bankrupted growth
reliant on high-octane humus, cleared canopy,
increased diversity and drainage,
promoting endangered meadow flowers.

Barbara, retired, organises weekday tours.

Rachel spends the snap of unrestricted days
between Christmas and New Year
processing through Heritage Lottery forms.

Students hop the wonky fence.
They spray graves with blood,
a sweet poisonous potion
of golden syrup, liquid soap and dye.

Poor Empress Barbara
borrows her husband's pocketknife,
stabs a coin-slot in a cashew tub
and strings it to the gatehouse door.

Rows of Differently Coloured Houses

By the sea, who was first
to buy their house a tin of yellow paint?
It stuck out like a golden tooth.
Then Captain's House went pink
and Belvedere turned green:
each street a string of plastic beads
and even when the sea's a rotten fish,
the town's as hopeful as a baby's quilt.

And here we are, on Megabus, curling
through the inland towns that didn't get a train
or sea, or any special scenery.
Lakes of postwar pebbledash
grey on grey on grey on grey.
Everyone hunched against the rain
as if it were a painful package, shouldered.

And if the borough council set aside
enough for everyone to pick a colour?

How dare you?
As if that's the problem!

Stegosaurus, primrose, marmalade,
strawberry, summer's day, champagne.

Stratigraphy

It's hard to be an archaeologist:
years of study, competition, applications
so you can kneel all day in the ground,
tugging the soil back one blanket at a time.

It's the only discipline that destroys the evidence as it goes.
Rates of sunburn and alcoholism are high.
And a trowel lasts at best a year
before the steel blade's worn away
in demonstration of what happens to the working hand.

Time doesn't always do its job.
I knew a guy: gave up digging
after clearing a churchyard in Kent.
A lead-lined coffin is better than Tupperware
and the child's face was perfect as a new bar of soap.

Duck

You teach children how to give.
They tear bread into damp-figured lumps
for you to shovel up in your snorkeling gear.

What excellent thrift
to make your feet from old umbrellas
and colour yourself with muesli,

to eat the river's beard
where it sprouts between the cold-washed scales
and to clean your own pond as you swim,
trailing a black ribbon through the glazed weed.

But though you can drag yourself up
and pass through the sky like a windscreen wiper
and your voice is loud enough to fill in the river,
you cannot stop the treading.

The banks grow lush with shame
as they stamp out the fire on your tail.

Starlings

We'd heard the fens were dying seas
pinned into their beds by reeds;
the sedges crowded out our path
through the washed-out winter marsh.

They came in ragged lines that fell
into the budding, chirping swell
of bodies caught up in a flow
that stretched itself like kneaded dough

until the churning shoal was black
and hemmed within a living sack
that smashed itself across the dusk
but could not break the thread of trust

that held each bird beside another
and pulled the molten flock together
until they turned and, plunging down,
were hooked into the weedy ground.

We both stood locked inside our coats
and in the dark we neither spoke
in case our clumsy blundering
upset the other's newfound wings.

Early Winter

It's not a frozen spoon on your tongue.
It's a mildew eating everything;
the path through the forest is pulp.

The trees weigh up the bad choice
and send a shunt to amputate each leaf.
A cataract ripens on the surface of the sun.

Still, the moss is more inviting now,
soft spires; we could curl down like mites.
The river flexes currents on its surface.

These assertions can be verified by anyone
with a car, or the leisure to daytrip by train,
or a little wood protected by a local council.

We're used to waiting winter out
like a debilitating cold. Our faith in spring
so strong we'd never call it faith.

It’s statistical analysis: every year we lived,
that year it came. These things can be predicted.
We read *FiveThirtyEight*. We know it comes:

it must. Or we’re stood in rotting undergrowth,
ankle deep in muck with mittened hands,
charged with shifting the axis of the earth.

Watching a North American Loon from St Thomas' Hospital

It mainly solves its problems
by not being there at all
but under water, coming up
in the smallest surface stitches.

I'm in a four-bed ward
and one of us just died.
They've closed the curtains
and sent in chatty students
with packets of digestives
to keep our minds away
from the removal.

So I decide *that*,
down there, is the descendent
of a North American Loon.
Look how it loops
under the white tourist cruiser.

In Alberta, a single pair
could rule a lake
the size of Westminster.

Here, her polka dot coat
is gravy stained with Thames water.

Any second,
she will shoot her call like a flare
and it will hang
over the office workers of Whitehall.

Hiding from a Mouse

Mia was late, so I opened up.
The mouse was on the kitchen step,
legs, flank and the side of his face
glued to a paper trap.

He looked so soft, strained to rise
then fell into himself, trying to catch
tiny shivering breaths.

He didn't have the purchase
of stump-legged pigeons
who tear their feet off to escape,
didn't have their weight.

I shut the kitchen door,
took the chairs down from the tables,
put out the thin glass pots of salt and pepper.

Mia made no fuss when she arrived:

drowned it in a saucepan.
She came from the former Yugoslavia;
to her we all seemed like children.

Offchurch

The wheat is ready for cropping, a full congregation
beside the road through the fields from nowhere to dismantled nowhere,
a brick bridge over a thirsty ditch and the cedar holding up its green tray
are the only telltales that there was once a big house that went on fire
or was sold in parts like a butchered cow and sometimes,
one evening in five, a car will crawl through to a corrugated farm.

And this is the only time you took the walk with me,
and because you were there and could charm a fish out of its pond
and make it want to stand on its tail to please you:
a saucer-faced barn owl pushed out from the stag oak,
boated into the blue for a moment, then dropped down into the corn.

I Have Chosen to Become a Plasterer

I want to smooth the world under light but firmly held tools.
I have practised by cutting bread without pressure on the knife:
just the brisk back and forth, allowing the thinnest slice
to curl away from the loaf like a fleece flap lolling back
as the farmer brings across the electrical shears.

My partner says I am sure to be a success.
He says the middle-classes love employing middle-classes,
that's why his parents got Bill the sculptor
to make their kitchen cupboard doors.

Explanation for Those Who Don't Know Love

I have a child and am more important
than childless people.

I am two people and have an extra vote.
You cannot comprehend our bond;

it is mysterious and I am greater because of it,
so in a tie-break situation I am three people.

My daughter is five and very bright for her age;
this requires special consideration.

She is a delight and centres every conversation
like a fantastic table decoration.

If she breaks your possessions
it's an interrogation of their meaning,

a state of blissful questioning you have lost.
If she cries it's only because she wants something.

She can't yet comprehend the magnitude of grief
so it is not selfish like when you cry.

Stay Home

Remember when we were flat hunting?
Our budget: ex-council, rented-rotten
and don't trust the gas certificate;
like what we thought we'd been living in.

There was that studenty mixed-doubles
with a rabbit stoppered in a hamster cage.
There were slim men asleep with rucksacks
and coats rolled on the ends of their beds.

I can't stop thinking of it.
That flat in Tower Hamlets where every wall
is bunks. So tight, two people on opposite sides
can touch knees across the gap.

Some beds are made with pillows at both ends.
Some beds have neatly bundled clothes
and a grungy dog or plastic horse tucked
where a grown-up sleeps round a child.

There are kids mute and staring at us
from the upper bunks, but the estate agent
keeps going like a pre-recorded tape.
There are adults folded away on their shelves,

a woman silently works the kitchenette,
and we can't get out fast enough.
I could whizz you up a metaphor,
a neat pun, appropriately shamed:

My stomach fills with fluid, legs with fluid,
still filling, so large, so disgustingly large
I could displace a mini-bus of people.
Stupid. Self-serving. I just needed to tell you,

again, what you certainly already know.
That in London, where they closed
Victoria Park and Brockwell Park,
people are living eight to a room.

On Follies

The best follies are built on a crest
and suggest a prow: the silk-sailed galleon
bearing through the blue behind them.

§

This vision wears its spiral stairs outside
with no handholds. At the top twist
steps are thinner than the slimmest hips
then narrow as one adult foot.
You will sidestep, nose scraping sandstone,
or choose outwards –
the trembling power of being held by nothing
and smooth cold at your back.
The turret is irresistible to local youths;
it propels their blood.

§

Structures measured in floors are not follies.
Follies rarely have roof gardens.
They're a carefully commissioned brooch
pinned on the breast of a well-maintained estate.
They don't need to bring their own
landscape in a doggie bag.

§

Stone stands. They require no maintenance;
window cleaners aren't winched down their sides.
There's no botched patching of aluminum frames.
If the rooves gape, they're picturesque.
If the walls sink, they're romantic.
They're mortal dreams, their fall imagined
even as they're built. Their decline hurts no one.

How to Balance Law Books on Your Head

The problem isn't *how*, I absolutely know
the answer is to go to Main Street,
some town I don't live, and find a stranger
who hates me, and my clothes, and my voice,
and who (while they would never dream
of hurting me in person) suspects
the world would be better with me dead,
and persuade her that she wants to stand
so close my greasy nose presses into hers
and, recycling each other's soupy breaths,
balance the books between us on our foreheads.
My only problem is how to do *that*.

Three King Canutes

The king, his gold retainers, a school of priests,
the men who can't remove their helmets
out of doors, and the plush unarmoured
cross a mirror-surfaced beach.

I

Laugh, laugh at the foolish fop-haired
Rollo square-face as he waves his sword,
slashes water, cold stung, face infection-hot
with tears, a mug in ruined boots.

II

The second king has quietness: a loved teacher
waiting for his class to own their error.
Surf nuzzles at his ankles.
This man's immovable, except a roll of hair
caught in the wind's chill currents and his eyes
resting in the eye of each advisor
until the sycophant wilts.

III

This last Canute has brought a camera crew.
His open suit and tie flap, the one concession
his women swapping heels for ballet pumps.
When water fills his shoes, it doesn't matter
he is rich and there are blankets in the waiting SUV.
He roars, *The waves will hold*,
as water's licking up his trouser legs.

He thinks he's in a story
and the better story wins.
That truth is just the story
that the audience lets in.

It doesn't matter if he's Cnut or Canute,
if we're in Norfolk or in Neverwhere.
He's miked up, entertaining,
and his wife's and daughter's hair
is sprayed as hard as bronze;
the wind, the sea, cannot mar the shot.

The Alibi

With thanks to B.H. who read many fourteenth- and fifteenth-century court documents in York Minster Library's records.

These three men claim their bosom friend
is not a bigamist. He didn't marry on that day.
They all went fishing. They remember this
perfectly because the not-husband
caught the largest trout they'd ever seen,
silver-plated flesh the length of your arm –
their whopper really was this big.

Good alibis are learned; no one's a natural.
Medieval men had no detective shows
to teach them how to mould a weekday lie
and the clerics found in favour of the wife.
But lucky us, our screens inform of more
than weddings whispered in a Yorkshire dark.

We're training from the day we're born,
and drill our skills to craft our masterpiece:

we were too young or far away,
we held no office relevant
to that particular atrocity.
We were on another continent.
We were needed in the office;
it was Adam's birthday and we all ate shortcake.

When I found some women with bellies

they were in the National Gallery
wearing dolphin-smooth skin
and only the airiest net at their hips,
stomachs round but childless,
snug with grapes and game.

Women with necks like glasses of milk
and naked jelly-mould breasts
carry confidence in their bellies.
If you plugged them to a socket
their abdomens would shine like bulbs.

Hilda and Cædmon

It isn't enough to turn snakes to stone;
miracles must be tidy, divinely mathematical.
So each spitting body she touched
rolled itself up in a ram's-horn curl.

When February storms
ploughed new steps in the beach,
fishermen found the frozen snakes
and split them for the jewels in their bellies.

She could steer the bishops in synod
like the farmer's wife who taught rabbits
to stand respectfully on Sundays.
She knew the price of wool.

Without her, he'd have been a shepherd
who once dreamt of a song and rolled it
round his mouth like an ear of pilfered wheat,
stilling his jaw when the overseer walked by.

Antonio, Duke of Milan

I was the one who met with generals,
negotiated pay and bonuses
to keep the city safe from our own men.

Everyday he made less effort
and bought more books.

Not that there weren't good ones:
An Atlas of the Indies, six feet long,
large enough to sit around at dinner.

Or a book of hours, size of an apricot,
more gold leaf than letters.
It took a monk sixteen years
on an island in the Northern sea
working each day except
when winter froze his ink.

But most had covers sagging off,

brown leper's skin;
he had them carried
through the city under escort
like statues of the Virgin during festivals.

I said, *You need to think about your people.*
But it was like he'd eaten all that dust.
His wife died and he didn't even notice.

Malcontents started to print pamphlets.
The Duke as a necromancer in long robes
talking to the Devil, lying with harlots.
I showed mercy, split a few nostrils,
cut off ears, but the damage was done.

By then he was mad.
He wanted a library,
a hall of books anyone could use.
We'd have the Papal armies on us in a month.

I said we couldn't afford it,
anyway we've printing presses now,
books are getting cheaper,

soon every house will have one.

But he said books were only half the point,
that people needed space to think,
went on about shared rooms where the baby's crying
and there's shouting through the walls.
As if those people read.

So I gave him space.

Put him on a boat and shipped him off,
although I let him have his wailing brat;
let him keep her dressed in white lace now.

Inheritance

To fight climate change, I can announce this government will institute 4 hours of community service per week, per man, and 7 hours and 12 minutes per woman.

At least that statement would be honest. No more pretending it's just a few more minutes, just a little bit more effort. That climate care can be achieved via a listicle of easy swaps.

And if you were to actually follow through? How many minutes per reusable nappy? And no tumble-drier, just winter babygrows over radiators like shucked skins. No sprays in bottle-guns, all soapy water and your elbow grease. Cloths not kitchen roll. Faffy washable food wraps. A bus to the bring-your-own-containers organic store, every moment weighing up which stranger you'll trust to hold your baby if someone needs the wheelchair space – it takes two hands to collapse your pram. Oh, it's so much healthier to cook from scratch. Make making the packed lunches therapeutic. Make do and mend. Trawl Freecycle and eBay in the evenings – it's like a game! The special bathroom bin houses the dark red odour of reusable sanitary items awaiting your attention.

I'm not saying this work doesn't need to be done, just that we need to be honest about who'll be doing it.

My mother out-law stares at me after this rant. She's so extraordinarily kind. Her face takes on a spongey look, maybe of a woman passing on an heirloom, maybe of a woman biting back, *What did you think we've been shouting all our lives?*

The Moon

The most hopeful item in the museum
is the medieval moon on a stick.

It's hollow, the size of a crystal ball,
and cups an economic candle.

It's made of smoky panes of horn
belted in a brass frame.

Riding at night, it bobs above your head,
a glowing balloon showing the way.

That metal thing on your hallway wall
is an artificial moon holder.

§

We're watching a Sunday tea-time adventure,
with archer outlaws or Tudor swagger,

when a coach bashes through forest
with torch-bearing outriders
or a drawbridge is bowed
for torch-waving henchmen
or extras revolt thrusting torches!

Why are these men burning tallow lollipops?
Can we have a scene before
where a woman wraps hours of hand-woven cloth,
made from afternoons of homespun thread,
and soaks it in enough pig fat to feed a family
all for it be set on fire?

When cheap glass lanterns
were as fantastical as fusion power
real people made the moon.

The Castle

Because horn lamps fell from fashion,
    we imagine naked flames.
Because wax-dipped linen perished,
    the windows had no panes.

Because coloured plaster crumbled
    there were granite window seats.
Because pastry's now a food-stuff
    we imagine fly-blown meats.

Because painted cloths don't last
    the servants shared this room.
Because tapestries are portable
    the walls were clotted gloom.

Because sweet-cut rushes rotted
    we assume the floors were bare.
Because they didn't live like us
    we find no comfort here.

The King's Manor Cat

Someone sent you a vase with a bulbed base,
round and weighty as a cantaloupe.

It smashed in the sorting office
and now the fragments
move inside the envelope so easily
the postman was able to force it
through your letter box, the wreckage
sliding like tectonic plates.

This is how we are born;
our skulls knit in our teens.
The grotesque movement enables safe delivery.

The problem is we risk sealing up completely.
The ossification continues like the famous cat
fed liver every elderly day until the vitamin A
fused it into one chalky block.

We must raise up the banners each morning
with the pulling back of the bedlinen.
We must not eat the liver.

England, Where Did You Go?

England of the burrow-in green, the chalk-galvanised giant,
undulating earth-bank fortress, the flinted Roman wall,
the full-flair gorse, messy hay-trails waiting
to be bin-bag-baled by steel mandibles:

you unroll through the window of a train,
but should I get out in search of you, you'd be off,
and I'd be left wandering down dual carriageways,
looking across bean fields and filthy ditches.

NOTES

DROUGHT. In many older versions of the St George and the Dragon story, the dragon nests on the town's only well. Maidens are sacrificed to lure the dragon away long enough for people to fetch water.

GARDEN CEMETERY TRUST. You know a Barbara and a Rachel. Tower Hamlets is one of the "Magnificent Seven" – a ring of Victorian cemeteries in the suburbs of London.

THE TRANSPORTATION OF GUANO. During the 19th cenutry large deposits of guano (up to 50 metres high) were mined in Peru, the Caribbean and Central Pacific atolls by slaves. This material was exported to the US and Europe as fertilizer.

EARLY WINTER. FiveThirtyEight is a blog edited by American statistician Nate Silver, which is known for accurate election predictions. The blog successfully predicted 49 out of 50 states in the 2008 US election and all 50 states in the 2012 election.

The night before the 2016 election FiveThirtyEight predicted Hillary Clinton had a 71% chance of winning. Predictions at the time included *New York Times* (85% Hillary to win), *Huffington Post* (98% Hillary to win), Predict Wise (89% Hillary to win), Princeton

Election Consortium (99% Hillary to win) and Daily Kos (92% Hillary to win).

STAY HOME. Victoria Park and Brockwell Park were closed in April 2020.

HILDA AND CÆDMON. Cædmon is traditionally celebrated as the first 'English Poet'. Cædmon became a monk supported by Hilda of Whitby, a noblewoman, an Abbess of a double monastery and later a saint. She was canonised for saving Whitby from an invasion of snakes, which she turned to stone. This miracle explains the large number of ammonites found in the area.

INHERITANCE. Women in the UK work 1.8 hours of unpaid domestic and care labour for every hour worked by men (Office for National Statistics).

THE MOON. "The moon was carried by servants to light their masters in lanes and dark roads, and could be used inside a house by fixing the pole into a socket. The moon was a 16th-century improvement on the cresset" – John Gloag, *A Short Dictionary of Furniture*.

THE CASTLE. Medieval pastry can be thought of as an equivalent of Tupperware. The purpose is to keep things air tight and you're not necessarily expected to eat the container. Painted cloths were used ubiquitously to subdivide and insulate spaces.

ACKNOWLEDGEMENTS

Thanks are due to the publications in which some of these poems first appeared: *The Poetry Review*, *Poetry London*, *Poetry Wales*, *The North*, *Five Dials*, *Poetry News*, *Magma*, *Verse Kraken*, *The Guernsey International Poetry Competition*, *Dear World & Everyone In It: New Poetry in the UK* (Bloodaxe Books), *Bedford Square 7* (Woodward Publishing), *Birdbook 1: Towns, Parks, Gardens and Woodlands* (Sidekick Books), *Other Countries: Contemporary Poets Rewiring History* (The Rewiring History Project), *Best Friends Forever: Poems on Female Friendship* (The Emma Press) and *Homesickness and Exile* (The Emma Press).

Thanks to Ann Sansom and everyone at Smith|Doorstop who published my pamphlet, *Soon Every House Will Have One*, where some of these poems were featured. I am also indebted to John McAuliffe who edited a selection of my work for *Carcanet New Poetries VIII*, and to Michael Schmidt and everyone at Carcanet.

I am grateful for the Hawthornden Fellowship and Eric Gregory Award that supported this work.

This collection was created over a long period and many people have given me feedback, advice and support along the way. Particular thanks are due to John Canfield, Angela Cleland, Dai George, Emily Hasler, Sarah Howe, Lynette Hunter, Rowena Knight, John McCullough, Kim Moore, JO Morgan, Abigail Parry, Kate Potts, Jon Stone and Alison Winch.

Beth Owen and Roddy Lumsden, thank you. I wish you could have seen this book.

Special thanks to my editor, Tom Chivers, for taking a chance on this work and this author. Thanks also to everyone at Penned in the Margins, especially Roisin Dunnett and Kate Wilkinson. Thanks to Zigmunds Lapsa for my stunning cover.

Thank you Alex, for understanding what's important.